LIFE PICTURE PUZZLE

WELCOME TO LIFE'S FIRST PICTURE PUZZLE BOOK

At the risk of blowing our own horn, it was not LIFE's intention to launch a wave of puzzlemania two years ago when we began publishing our back-page Picture Puzzle each Friday. We were simply trying to create a diversion that readers could enjoy for a few minutes together at the family breakfast table, pencils in hand. It seems that we somewhat underestimated just how popular the puzzles would be. By an incredibly wide margin.

From the very first day of publication, we received letters from people telling us how much they enjoyed solving the puzzles, pleading for more, and divulging how they couldn't wait for next week's to arrive. Six-year-olds sent us completed puzzles annotated in crayon. Eighty-year-olds sent e-mails begging us to *please* raise the difficulty level once in a while. Law-enforcement agencies asked if they could use the puzzles to help train new recruits. (We said yes.)

As the months passed, hundreds of readers wrote us asking the same question: Is there a book of Picture Puzzles for sale? Well, now there is. This is the first of what LIFE hopes will be many Picture Puzzle books. This isn't a collection of previously published brainteasers—none of the 90 puzzles contained between these two covers has appeared elsewhere. Devoted puzzlers, renowned for their sharp eyes, will recognize some photos that have been previously published in LIFE. These have been reworked with all-new clues. They'll also notice that some pictures repeat two or three times within the book, in slightly different forms. Each is a distinct puzzle, with its own set of alterations to spot.

If you're a fan of the LIFE Picture Puzzle, you'll notice that we've expanded the usual format. Puzzles are categorized into four levels of difficulty: novice, master, expert, and genius. For those who like to race against the clock, we've also added a suggested completion time. Answers, which in the magazine appear at the bottom of the puzzle page, are located at the back of this book. This is to discourage peeking. (You culprits know who you are.) Fans of the classic format can still find a brand-new puzzle every week on the back page of LIFE and a growing archive of them at *www.LIFE.com.* We'd love to know what you think of the book. If you get a chance, drop us a note at picturepuzzle@life.com. In the meantime, enjoy!

Secret puzzle bonus! We've concealed 10 secret changes in the puzzles within this book. Think you've found one? Log on to *www.LIFE.com/Life/extra_answers* to find out! In addition, we've hidden two more puzzles on our Web site, but you can reach them only through the private entrance: Go to *www.LIFE.com* and click PICTURE PUZZLE. On the next page, click the second *Z* in the word PUZZLE, whisper "Open sesame," and *ta-da!*

[HOW TO PLAY THE PUZZLES]

Fancy Footwork

Sweat the details a bit on this, and you'll have a ball

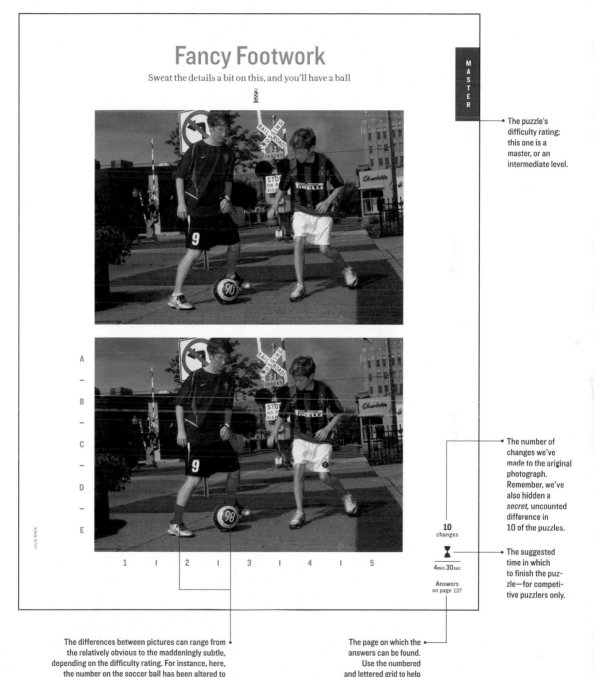

MASTER

The puzzle's difficulty rating; this one is a master, or an intermediate level.

The number of changes we've made to the original photograph. Remember, we've also hidden a *secret*, uncounted difference in 10 of the puzzles.

10 changes

The suggested time in which to finish the puzzle—for competitive puzzlers only.

4min 30sec

Answers on page 137

The differences between pictures can range from the relatively obvious to the maddeningly subtle, depending on the difficulty rating. For instance, here, the number on the soccer ball has been altered to read 98 instead of 90, and he's put on new socks. Eight more changes are left to spot in this one.

The page on which the answers can be found. Use the numbered and lettered grid to help you find any changes you might have missed.

LIFE PICTURE PUZZLE

Editor Mark Adams
Designer Jarred Ford
Photo Editor Caroline Smith
Copy Chief Danielle Dowling
Production Manager Michael Roseman
Research Editor Damien McCaffery
Associate Production Manager Rachel Hendrick
Puzzle Consultants Alex Adams, Stephanie Fletcher, Tosca LaBoy, Adam Raymond
Contributors Katherine Bigelow, Marina Drukman, Kate Rope
Contributing Puzzle Photographer Julie Mack

LIFE Magazine
Managing Editor Bill Shapiro
Creative Director Richard Baker
Executive Editorial Manager Maura Fritz
Director of Photography George Pitts
Art Director Bess Wong

LIFE Books
President Andrew Blau
Business Manager Roger Adler
Business Development Manager Jeff Burak
Editorial Director Robert Sullivan

Editorial Operations Richard K. Prue, David Sloan (DIRECTORS),
Richard Shaffer (GROUP MANAGER), Burt Carnesi, Brian Fellows, Raphael Joa,
Angel Mass, Stanley E. Moyse (MANAGERS), Soheila Asayesh, Keith Aurelio,
Trang Ba Chuong, Ellen Bohan, Charlotte Coco, Osmar Escalona, Kevin Hart,
Norma Jones, Mert Kerimoglu, Rosalie Khan, Marco Lau, Po Fung Ng, Rudi Papiri,
Barry Pribula, Carina A. Rosario, Albert Rufino, Christopher Scala, Vaune Trachtman,
Paul Tupay, Lionel Vargas, David Weiner

Time Inc. Home Entertainment
Publisher Richard Fraiman
Executive Director, Marketing Services Carol Pittard
Director, Retail & Special Sales Tom Mifsud
Marketing Director, Branded Businesses Swati Rao
Director, New Product Development Peter Harper
Financial Director Steven Sandonato
Book Production Manager Jonathan Polsky
Marketing Manager Laura Adam
Manager, Prepress & Design Anne-Michelle Gallero

Special thanks to Bozena Bannett, Alexandra Bliss, Glenn Buonocore,
Suzanne Janso, Robert Marasco, Brooke McGuire, Chavaughn Raines,
Mary Sarro-Waite, Ilene Schreider, Adriana Tierno

PUBLISHED BY

LIFE BOOKS

Vol.6, No.2 • November 2006

If you would like to order any of our hardcover Collector's Edition books, please call us
at 800-327-6388. (Monday through Friday, 7 a.m. to 8 p.m., or Saturday, 7 a.m. to
6 p.m. Central Time).
Please visit us, and sample past editions of LIFE, at *www.LIFE.com*.

READY, SET, GO!

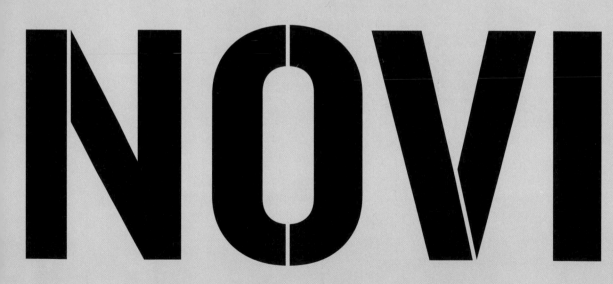

These puzzles are for everyone:
rookies and veterans,
young and old. Start here, and
sharpen your skills.

Just a Hop, Skip, and a Jump

How much busier (and sillier) is the picture at right than the
one below? We'll let you count the ways.

A

B

C

D

E

1   2   3   4   5

9
changes

2min 30sec

Answers
on page 137

Say *Arrrrrgh!*

Yes, matey, this one's just a wee bit tougher than the last—but surely a buccaneer with your skills can unearth the treasures we've buried

A
—
B
—
O
—
D
—
E

1   2   3   4   5

8
changes

⏳
2min 45sec

Answers
on page 137

Flight Change

Without delay, try to spot all the ways these photos aren't uniform

✈

7
changes

⏳

3min 15sec

Answers
on page 137

A

B

C

D

E

1 2 3 4 5

Will You Make the Cut?

Only the sharpest puzzlers can solve this one. See if you're one of them.

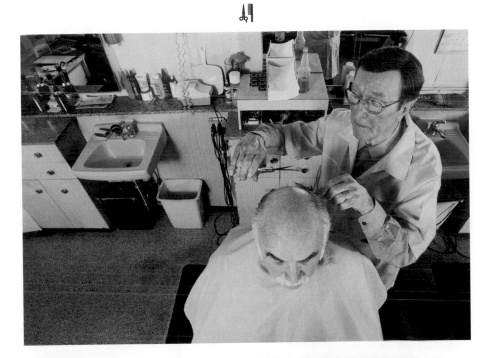

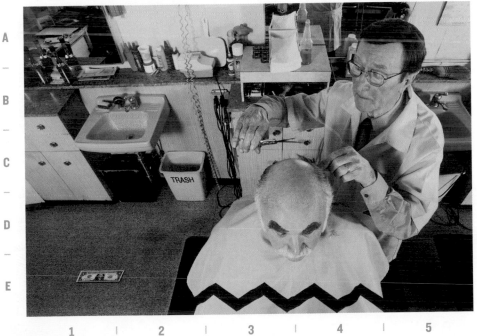

A
—
B
—
C
—
D
—
E

1   2   3   4   5

7
changes

2 min 30 sec

Answers
on page 137

Pool Shark

Things are just getting interesting in this backyard. Look closely,
and you'll notice some new developments.

A

B

C

D

E

1   2   3   4   5

6 changes

⏳ 2min 40sec

Answers on page 137

Read Between the Lines

Five of these pictures are identical. One is slightly different.
See if you can ID the impostor.

0min **35**sec

Answer
on page 137

The Table's New Contents

These photos all feature the same menu—except for the one in which we've ordered up something extra

1

2

3

4

5

6

0min 30sec

Answer
on page 137

Get Your Kicks

You'll have a ball with this puzzle if you keep one goal in mind—
to find the differences between these photos

A
–
B
–
C
–
D
–
E

1   2   3   4   5

7
changes

⧗
2min 45sec

Answers
on page 137

Why Write This One Off?

Just because things have been deducted, added, and otherwise altered in this photo

A
–
B
–
C
–
D
–
E

8
changes

⏳

2min 0sec

Answers
on page 137

1   2   3   4   5

Honk if You Love Bananas

And flash your high beams when you've found the changes

6
changes

2min **10**sec

Answers
on page 137

Don't Miss the Bus

Or we'll have to mark you down as tardy in spotting the differences

7
changes

⏳
3min 55sec

Answers
on page 137

Extra Carrots, Anyone?

Good, because there are plenty of them—and other surprises—in these pictures

7 changes

⏳

4min 15sec

Answers on page 137

A
B
C
D
E

1   2   3   4   5

Take Your Best Shot

A pro like you should nail this one

A

—

B

—

C

—

D

—

E

1   2   3   4   5

8
changes

3min 15sec

Answers
on page 138

You're Getting Warmer

Here's an industrial-strength puzzler for you—find the differences between one picture and the other (and keep an eye on the gauge)

A
B
C
D
E

1 2 3 4 5

7
changes

3min 40sec

Answers
on page 138

Flower Fiesta

Let's get this garden party started. Anyone want to change clothes first?

A
—
B
—
C
—
D
—
E

6
changes

⧖

1min 15sec

Answers
on page 138

1   2   3   4   5

Secret Recipe

Shhh! There are a few ingredients these photos don't share. What are they?

A
—
B
—
C
—
D
—
E

1   2   3   4   5

6
changes

2min 30sec

Answers
on page 138

Mere Child's Play

This one's so easy, even a grown-up could do it.
(No asking a kid for help—that's cheating.)

8
changes

⏳

2min 50sec

Answers
on page 138

How Sharp Are You?

All you need to solve this one is a really big pencil. *Hmm.*

A —

B —

C —

D —

E —

8
changes

1min 55sec

Answers
on page 138

1   2   3   4   5

Where There's Smoke

Both of these photos are hot, but one positively sizzles. Which?

8
changes

2min 50sec

Answers
on page 138

Ready to Burst?

Don't explode yet. Wait until you've finished this puzzle.

A

B

C

D

E

1　　　2　　　3　　　4　　　5

10
changes

⏳

3min 0sec

Answers
on page 138

Easter Surprise

One of these pictures is a bit different from the rest. See if you can find it.

1

2

3

4

5

6

1min 5sec

Answer
on page 138

School, Yes. Uniform, No.

Which of these photos is not quite like the others?

1

2

3

4

5

6

1min 0sec

Answer
on page 138

Bunky
$9.99 lb.

A

B

C

D

E

1   2   3   4   5

8
changes

4min 15sec

Answers
on page 138

Seeing Double?

Then you're off to a good start. Keep going.

8
changes

1min 50sec

Answers
on page 138

A

B

C

D

E

1   2   3   4   5

Houston, I'll Have a Sandwich

Don't space out just *yet*—this one's a blast!

★ ★ ★

7
changes

3min 30sec

Answers
on page 139

A
B
C
D
E

1   2   3   4   5

Give Yourself a Star . . .

. . . if you can spot all the variations between these pictures

8
changes

5min 30sec

Answers
on page 139

Watching Grass Grow

Spot all the changes first, and make your friends green with envy

A
–
B
–
C
–
D
–
E

7
changes

3min 0sec

Answers
on page 139

1   2   3   4   5

You're on a Roll

Don't let this deceptively easy-looking puzzle slow you down

7
change**s**

2 min 10 se c

Answers
on page 139

Are You Seeing Spots?

Good, because you'll find a swarm of them in these pictures.
Can you find the differences between the two?

A
–
B
–
C
–
D
–
E

1   2   3   4   5

6
changes

⌛
4min 0sec

Answers
on page 139

What's the Big Hurry?

There are plenty of things to look for in this puzzle. Take your time, stay dry, and keep a close watch on any and all stripes.

A

B

C

D

E

1 2 3 4 5

10
changes

⏳
4min 25sₑ

Extra Credit

You'll notice that a student in one of these photos got an A+. Will you too?

MUSIC CLASS
3:00

15
changes

⏳
6min 0sec

ER[ ]

Here, puzzles get
a little harder. You'll
need to raise
your game a level.

Howdy, Puzzle Pardner

Before you git along to the next brainteaser, why not stop at this li'l cowpoke's birthday party? And round up a posse to find the changes we've made to this here photo.

A

–

B

–

C

–

D

–

E

1   I   2   I   3   I   4   I   5

10
changes

7min 5sec

Answers
on page 139

Office Work

This person has stepped out, but there's plenty left to do. For starters:
The differences between these photos need to be found.

A
–
B
–
C
–
D
–
E

1 | 2 | 3 | 4 | 5

8
changes

3min 0sec

Answers
on page 139

Do You Need Glasses?

This guy might if he keeps losing his. (A tip: Check the shelf first.)

A

—

B

—

C

—

D

—

E

8 changes

6min 30sec

Answers on page 139

1   2   3   4   5

Something's Missing Here

And it's not just the ocean, dude

A

—

B

—

C

—

D

—

E

1 | 2 | 3 | 4 | 5

8
changes

4min 15sec

Answers
on page 139

Special Order

One of these tables has a flavor that the others lack. Can you identify it?

1min 30sec

Answer
on page 140

Find Everything You Need?

See how quickly you can *spot* the unique picture

1

2

3

4

5

6

1min 15sec

Answer
on page 140

Kitchen Confidential

Can you keep a secret? While the cookie recipes on these pages are identical, the photos aren't.

9
changes

4min 0sec

Answers
on page 140

Don't Bug Out

It's not quite as hard as it looks, if you remember to connect the dots

A
—
B
—
C
—
D
—
E

1   2   3   4   5

7
changes

⏳

3min 15sec

Answers
on page 140

And Don't Go Off the Deep End

Immerse yourself in this puzzle, and the differences will start to surface

7
changes

5min 25sec

Answers
on page 140

Picnic Puzzler

After you've found all the changes, do not go swimming for at least 30 minutes

A

—

B

—

C

—

D

—

E

8
changes

2min 45sec

Answers
on page 140

1　I　2　I　3　I　4　I　5

Luggage Mix-Up

See if you can sort out the chaos at this airport

7
changes

2min 15sec

Answers
on page 140

A Real Eye-Opener

These pictures appear to be the same, but take a second look

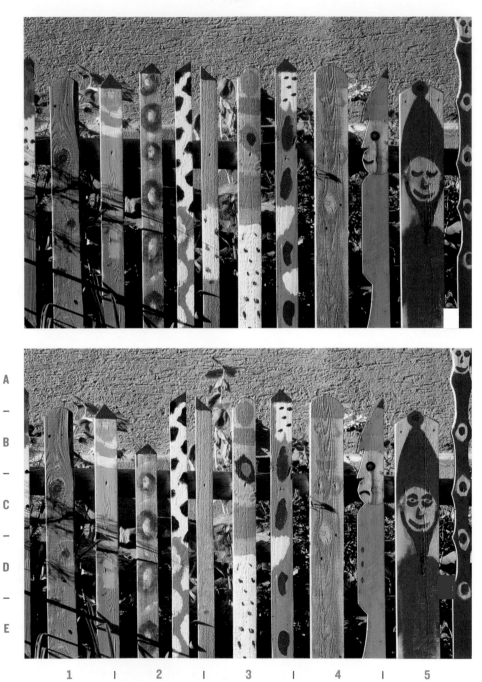

8
changes

4min **55**sec

Answers
on page 140

A — B — C — D — E

1 | 2 | 3 | 4 | 5

Dad, Did You See That?

This one's sneaky, so pause for a moment of reflection (hint, hint)

7
changes

⏳

3min **35**sec

Answers
on page 140

Here's a Hot One

Don't stop now, you're on fire! Finish this puzzle in less than the allotted time, and someone might have to hose you off.

A

–

B

–

C

–

D

–

E

1   2   3   4   5

10
changes

⏳
3min 10sec

Answers
on page 140

Unexplained Phenomena

You don't have to believe in ghosts to see there's something spooky going on here

10
changes

⧗
7min 0sec

Answers
on page 140

Watch for Signs

They, and a few other things, might change if you don't keep an eye on them

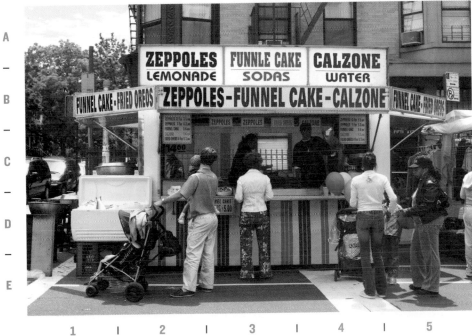

8
changes

4min 0sec

Answers
on page 140

Lost in Translation

There are a few *diferencias* between these two *fotos*. Can you spot them all? *¡Por supuesto!*

A
—
B
—
C
—
D
—
E

1   2   3   4   5

8
changes

5min 15sec

Answers
on page 141

What's Cooking Here?

Only the shadow knows (that's your tip-off). Might want to start at the bottom with this one.

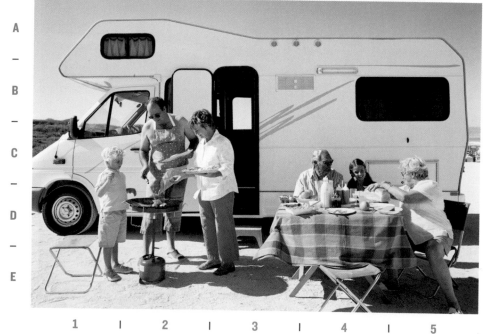

8 changes

5min 30sec

Answers on page 141

Slumber Party

Don't let this one keep you up all night—take a good look at those backpacks

A
—
B
—
C
—
D
—
E

1 | 2 | 3 | 4 | 5

7
changes

5min 0sec

Answers
on page 141

Only the Hose Knows

We buried some strange additions, subtractions, and other oddities
in this lady's street garden. How many can you dig up?

A

—

B

—

C

—

D

—

E

1   2   3   4   5

7
changes

4min **15**sec

Answers
on page 141

It All Comes Out in the Wash

Maybe there's soap in our eyes, but these pictures look different. Can you count the ways?

A
–
B
–
C
–
D
–
E

8
changes

6min 0sec

Answers
on page 141

1 | 2 | 3 | 4 | 5

Look What I Found!

Do a little snooping around to see what you can turn up too

A
—
B
—
C
—
D
—
E

1   2   3   4   5

7
changes

5min 15sec

Answers
on page 141

A Nice, Neat Row

Everything appears to be in order here—except for the bunch of modifications we've made. Can you pick them out?

A

B

C

D

E

1 | 2 | 3 | 4 | 5

8
changes

⧖
7min 30sec

Answers
on page 141

Don't Flake Out

At least not until you see what's different in these photos. Get the drift?

8
changes

3min **0**sec

Answers
on page 141

A
—
B
—
C
—
D
—
E

1 | 2 | 3 | 4 | 5

Under Achievers

Search high. Search low. Find the changes, then on you go.

☺

A
—
B
—
C
—
D
—
E

1 | 2 | 3 | 4 | 5

8
changes

⏳

5min 5sec

Answers
on page 141

Heavy Lifting

Things are on the move at this shipping yard—see if you can keep track of them

A
—
B
—
C
—
D
—
E

1 | 2 | 3 | 4 | 5

11
changes

⧗

8min 50sec

Answers
on page 141

Grin and Bear It

These creatures are cuddly, this puzzle is less so. Approach with caution.

8 changes

⏳ 8min 0sec

Answers on page 141

Rain, Rain, Go Away

We can't change the weather, but we did alter one of these photos. Can you find it?

2min 20sec

Answer
on page 142

Which Witch Is Which?

One of these Halloween scenes is unlike the others. Don't be spooked
if it takes you a while to recognize the impostor.

1

2

3

4

5

6

0min 45sec

Answer
on page 142

Tool Time

Somebody's been messing around in this workshop and has made a few changes. You know the drill.

A

B

C

D

E

1 | 2 | 3 | 4 | 5

9
changes

⏳
4min 40sec

Answers
on page 142

Try This On for Size

This is a big one, so catch your breath and pour yourself a beverage. Ready? Go.

15
changes

⧗
10min 0sec

Answers
on page 142

RT [

Only serious puzzlers
dare to tread past this point.
Who's in?

]

Buoy, That's a Tough One

These marine floatables look pretty similar, but if you compare the
two photos, you might discover differences

A

B

C

D

E

1 | 2 | 3 | 4 | 5

9
changes

7min 0sec

Answers
on page 142

Chango of Style

There's a trend afoot here: You'll get a kick out of these ever-changing patterns

A

—

B

—

C

—

D

—

E

8
changes

⧗

7 min 50 sec

Answers
on page 142

1   2   3   4   5

This One's No Picnic

Except for a pro like you. Don't forget to, ahem, *check* the tablecloth, champ.

8
changes

6 min 50 sec

Answers
on page 142

Flying Colors

You won't need a magnifying glass for this one. But reading glasses wouldn't hurt.

9 changes

8min 55sec

Answers on page 142

A

B

C

D

E

1 2 3 4 5

What Are You Two Hiding?

For such a sweet couple, these two sure do make a mean puzzle

♥

A
—
B
—
C
—
D
—
E

1   2   3   4   5

9
changes

⧗

8min 30sec

Answers
on page 142

Make a Wish

One of these birthday photos doesn't quite fit in.
Can you spot the party crasher?

1

2

3

4

5

6

⧗ 2min 5sec

Answer
on page 142

Find the Spare Change

Here's the $64,000 question: Which of the following photos has been altered slightly?

1

2

3

4

5

6

2min 30sec

Answer
on page 142

Squeeze Play

There's a wagonload of differences between these pictures. How many can you find?

A
—
B
—
C
—
D
—
E

9
changes

⧗
6min 35sec

Answers
on page 143

1   2   3   4   5

Take a Fresh Look

This puzzle isn't just good fun—it's good *for* you

A

B

C

D

E

1   2   3   4   5

8
changes

7min **55**sec

Answers
on page 143

Easter Egg Hunt

Keep your nose to the ground, and perhaps you'll root out the changes

A

B

C

D

E

1   2   3   4   5

9
changes

⏳

10min 45sec

Answers
on page 143

What's Up, Dock?

A serious puzzle contender like you should have no problem locating
the tiny discrepancies we've loaded into these two pictures

1   2   3   4   5

10
changes

⏳
9min 0sec

Answers
on page 143

Garden of Surprises

If you can cut through the foliage, you might like what you find in here

A   B   C   D   E

1   2   3   4   5

11
changes

⧖
8min 10sec

Answers
on page 143

Fully Loaded

There's a lot of stuff in these two cars, not all of it the same. What's different?

8
changes

9min **20**sec

Answers
on page 143

A

B

C

D

E

1   2   3   4   5

You'd Better Not Cry

We're telling you why: Because Santa wants you to solve this puzzle

A
—
B
—
C
—
D
—
E

1   2   3   4   5

9
changes

⏳

12min **30**sec

Answers
on page 143

The Party's Over

But the puzzle fun continues. Notice anything new here?

8
changes

⏳

6min 10sec

Answers
on page 143

A

B

C

D

E

1   2   3   4   5

Pick Up the Tempo

You've found your rhythm—now step to it and start searching

A
—
B
—
C
—
D
—
E

1 | 2 | 3 | 4 | 5

8
changes

9min **35**sec

Answers
on page 143

Pouring It On

Is this one a little tougher than usual? Sure. But chances are good that you're a budding champion.

A

B

C

D

E

1 2 3 4 5

10
changes

⧗
13min 30sec

Answers
on page 143

More Fun Than a Movie

The offerings at your typical theater's concession stand are fairly standard, but a
discerning customer will note some differences between these two

A
–
B
–
C
–
D
–
E

1 | 2 | 3 | 4 | 5

10
changes

⧗
7min 45sec

Answers
on page 144

One Tough Cookie

How much dough would you be willing to bet that you can solve this one?

A B C D E

1 2 3 4 5

11 changes

⏳ 12min 15sec

Answers on page 144

Sink or Swim

You may feel like you're paddling upstream, so here's a hint: Watch the toys

A   B   C   D   E

1   2   3   4   5

10 changes

8min 5sec

Answers on page 144

Finding a single difference in these puzzles is a challenge. Finding them all might be impossible.

This Paint's Been Mixed

Clear the spots out of your eyes—you'll need to look sharp to find which of these photos is slightly different from the rest

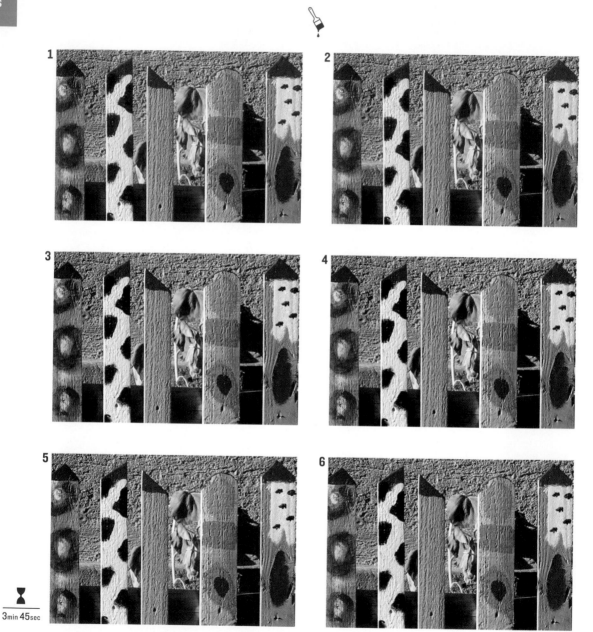

3min 45sec

Answer
on page 144

Can You Catch It?

There's one oddball photo in the six shown.
A hint: Something has grown.

GENIUS

1

2

3

4

5

6

4min 10sec

Answer on page 144

A Little Bit of Everything

Here's one occasion when your eyes *should* be bigger than your stomach

A
—
B
—
C
—
D
—
E

1   2   3   4   5

10
changes

⏳

6min 20sec

Answers
on page 144

Race Against Time

Ladies and gentlemen, start your pencils

A
—
B
—
C
—
D
—
E

1   2   3   4   5

8
changes

5min 10sec

Answers
on page 144

Now Things Get Interesting

Can't lie to you: This one is quite difficult. Find all the changes, and you truly are a genius.

5

4

3

2

1

A

B

C

D

E

10
changes

16min 40sec

Answers
on page 144

One Really Hard Bargain

Attention, shoppers! This puzzle is extremely challenging. Check every reflection, box, and sign.

A | B | C | D | E

1 | 2 | 3 | 4 | 5

10
changes

18min 0sec

Answers
on page 144

Final Exam

It all comes down to this: Find 10, and you're good; find all 20, and you're at the head of the class

5

4

3

2

1

A — B — C — D — E

20
changes

20min 0sec

Answers
on page 144

Finished already? Let's see how you did.

[INTRODUCTION]

Page 3: **Fancy Footwork** No. 1 (A4): One arm of the crossing sign has grown skyward. No. 2 (A5): Old Glory now flies atop the building. No. 3 (B3): The sign says NO instead of ON. No. 4 (C1): Caution! Red lights flashing! No. 5 (C3): The car has disappeared. No. 6 (C4): His shorts have a logo to match his shirt's. No. 7 (C5): The fence has been extended to the sidewalk. No. 8 (D3 and E2): He's changed his socks. No. 9 (E1): Some of the shadow is gone. No. 10 (E3): The ball's O has become an 8.

[NOVICE]

Page 8: **Just a Hop, Skip, and a Jump** No. 1 (A1): The new chimney's arrived. No. 2 (A3): Three of the white boards under the eaves are gone. No. 3 (B3): The window has eight panes. No. 4 (C1): Change of address—it's now 13. No. 5 (C2): Needles make swell hairpins. No. 6 (D1 to E1): Hopscotch, anyone? No. 7 (E3): That red yarn should come in handy. No. 8 (E4): White socks suit you, sir. No. 9 (E5): Don't spill that gigantic mug of coffee.

Page 10: **Say Arrrrrrgh!** No. 1 (A3): The pirate's patch has switched eyes. No. 2 (B1): The palm leaves blew away. No. 3 (B3): His (swash)buckle has slid down. No. 4 (B5 to C5): No more window view for you, cap'n. No. 5 (D4): A house has disappeared. No. 6 (D5): She's having double the fun. No. 7 (E3): Wait—are they playing miniature football? No. 8 (E4): Or is it, er, baseball?

Page 12: **Flight Change** No. 1 (B3 to C3): Her scarf is twice as large. And twice as pretty. Nos. 2 and 3 (C1): Hey, who's that guy in the window? Sure hope the flight hasn't taken off already. And note that she went with the blue shirt instead of the white. No. 4 (C5): He's earned some extra stripes. No. 5 (D2): Her coffee cup has been filled. No. 6 (D4 to E4): His tie's been dotted. No. 7 (E4): Apparently his name is really ALEX.

Page 13: **Will You Make the Cut?** No. 1 (B1): The sink has water in it. No. 2 (C2): Hey, that receptacle is for TRASH. No. 3 (C3 to D3): The phone cord dangles to the floor. No. 4 (C4): His tie has turned red. No. 5 (D3 to D4): Might want to trim those eyebrows next. No. 6 (E1): Somebody's dropped a dollar. No. 7 (E2 to E4): His smock looks like Charlie Brown's shirt. Rats!

Page 14: **Pool Shark** No. 1 (C1): There's a new duck in town. No. 2 (C2 to E1): The yellow and the blue on the paddle have switched places. No. 3 (C4): Now *that* is a big horse. No. 4 (D2): The boat's been christened the S.S. *Minnow*. No. 5 (D3): The valve has disappeared. No. 6 (D5): Shark!

Page 16: **Read Between the Lines** In photo No. 3, the fuchsia T-shirt has white stripes.

Page 17: **The Table's New Contents** The saltshaker in photo No. 4 now says SALT.

Page 18: **Get Your Kicks** No. 1 (A1): His new jersey reads ERNESTO. No. 2 (A3): He now has a wristband. No. 3 (B2): His shorts have gone from 6 to 9. No. 4 (C4): The red center stripe has gone gray. No. 5 (D1): His sock has turned white. No. 6 (D2): The soccer ball looks happy. No. 7 (D5): That glove has his hand covered. **Did you find the secret bonus difference?** If not, log on to *www.LIFE.com* to find out what it is.

Page 20: **Why Write This One Off?** No. 1 (A4): The phone is upside down. No. 2 (B2): That carrot looks tasty. No. 3 (B4 to C4): Her collar has turned white. No. 4 (C3): That's sure a big jar—must be megavitamins. No. 5 (C5): Her chair's open back has been filled in. No. 6 (D2): His mug just *loves* New York! No. 7 (D3): She's off coffee and on grape juice. No. 8 (E4): The table has lost a leg.

Page 21: **Honk if You Love Bananas** No. 1 (B2): Can *you* balance an orange on your head? No. 2 (B3): The scale is filled with grapes. No. 3 (B4): The taxi has lost its roof light. No. 4 (C1): Wow, that's a lot of bananas. No. 5 (D5): The brown box is now bright yellow. No. 6 (E4): Look at that cute little fire truck.

Page 22: **Don't Miss the Bus** No. 1 (A1): Good morning, moon! No. 2 (A2): Let's go—the light has turned green. No. 3 (B2): A building has vanished. No. 4 (B3 to C3): So have some windows. No. 5 (C3): The sign says COOL BUS. No. 6 (E2): The front hubcap is now a matching yellow. No. 7 (E4): Someone has painted lane lines on the street. **Did you find the secret bonus difference?** If not, log on to *www.LIFE.com* to find out what it is.

Page 24: **Extra Carrots, Anyone?** No. 1 (A5): That window is a whole lot bigger. No. 2 (B1): His suspenders have turned black. No. 3 (B3 to C3): Her blouse has lost its print. No. 4 (D2): A milk jug is upside down. No. 5 (D3): The coffeepot has fallen over. No. 6 (D4 to D5): The large container is now blue. No. 7 (E5): A second bowl of carrots has appeared. Yum!

Page 25: **Take Your Best Shot**
No. 1 (A5): That scale is worth its weight in gold. No. 2 (B3): Wave that flag, dude! No. 3 (B5): Where'd the net go? No. 4 (C1): One of those desk legs is not like the others. No. 5 (C2): My, how your beard has grown. No. 6 (C5): The tread on his sneaker has changed. No. 7 (D3): The name JOSHUA has appeared on a piece of paper. No. 8 (E5): The framed picture on his desk has been blown up.

Page 26: **You're Getting Warmer** No. 1 (A1 to A2): *Hmm*, 98.6 seems a little high for that gauge. No. 2 (A2 to A5): The cable has gone from blue to yellow. No. 3 (B2): Did someone order coffee? No. 4 (C3): Another hole has appeared. No. 5 (C5): The valve has been turned. No. 6 (D1): Caution! No. 7 (D3): Sometimes you just *don't* feel like a nut.

Page 28: **Flower Fiesta** No. 1 (B2): The yellow flower is now a daisy. No. 2 (B4): His helmet has been painted red. No. 3 (C4): His shorts have gone from patterned to plain. No. 4 (D2): The brown horse has turned white. No. 5 (E1): Gee, that's a big pinecone. No. 6 (E5): Hello, kitty!

Page 29: **Secret Recipe** No. 1 (A1 to C1): Let's hope they didn't need anything in that cabinet—it's gone. No. 2 (A3): Mom's new brown hair looks nice. No. 3 (C4): Her apron's been dyed red. No. 4 (D2): There's an extra egg atop the oatmeal. No. 5 (E4): The red and the green panels on the peanut butter label have swapped places. No. 6 (E5): Get ready for a really big (chocolate) Kiss! **Did you find the secret bonus difference? If not, log on to** *www.LIFE.com* **to find out what it is.**

Page 30: **Mere Child's Play** No. 1 (A4): Are you kids supposed to be reading after dark? No. 2 (A5): Cake's done! No. 3 (B1): That stuffed dog is not quite Clifford-sized, but it sure got big. No. 4 (B2): Her collar is now striped instead of dotted. No. 5 (B3): His buttons are black. No. 6 (B4): Someone's left the water on. No. 7 (D3): He needed a Band-Aid. No. 8 (D5): The dog's spotty face has cleared up.

Page 32: **How Sharp Are You?**
No. 1 (A5): Here comes an airplane! No. 2 (B1): That tower has undergone a little altitude adjustment. No. 3 (B2 to C5): Is that a rocket or a pencil? No. 4 (B3): On second thought, make it a super-duper-jumbo burger. No. 5 (C2): Where'd the ASTROLAND sign go? Maybe you can ask Roland. No. 6 (C4): The Italian sausage sign is upside down. Nos. 7 and 8 (E2): Now *which* way are the bathrooms? And, my, that's a bright green shirt.

Page 33: **Where There's Smoke**
No. 1 (A4): Up, periscope! No. 2 (B1): Oh, are we doing some lawn bowling? No. 3 (C3): That polite boy has cleared his plate. Nos. 4 and 5 (C5): One fellow has a 5 on his back, and another has a new hatband. No. 6 (D1): Her plate's looking sort of yellow. No. 7 (D2): Burger, anyone? No. 8 (D4): Her shoes are now black.

Page 34: **Ready to Burst?** No. 1 (A1): Yikes, that's a huge snowflake. Nos. 2 and 3 (A3): He's found another balloon. Yay! And his hair is pink. Double yay! No. 4 (B4): A sparkly snowflake has melted away. *Booo!* No. 5 (B5): Howdeedo, happy star. No. 6 (C3): His shirt is covering his tummy. No. 7 (C5 to D5): Whose handprint is that? No. 8 (E2): A balloon now reads HAPPY NEW YEAR! No. 9 (E3): His socks match his new hair. No. 10 (E4): Another blue balloon. Yay!

Page 36: **Easter Surprise** Photo No. 6 is the oddball—the bunny slipper at right has had a little work done.

Page 37: **School, Yes. Uniform, No.** Picture No. 2 shows the bus with its top lights on.

Page 38: **Like a Kid in a Candy Store**
No. 1 (A2): We don't know who Bunky is, but he costs $9.99 a pound. No. 2 (B1): The lemon-lime candy has become more patriotic. No. 3 (B2 to C2): His shirt's cowboy hat is upside down. His stomach's going to be, too, if he keeps eating that candy. No. 4 (B4): There was a run on orange sherbert, apparently. No. 5 (C4): The pink and the blue on her shirt have been reversed. No. 6 (D2): Young man, where did you get those extra jelly beans? No. 7 (D3): That is one big, black Jelly Belly. No. 8 (E3): Someone's spilled the beans! Bunky, probably.

Page 40: **Seeing Double?** No. 1 (A2 to A5): The sky has turned gray. Sure looks like a storm's blowing in. No. 2 (A4): That girl is pulling off quite a balancing act. No. 3 (B1 to C2): Hey, close the shutters—rain's on the way! No. 4 (C1): It seems showers have brought more flowers. No. 5 (C5): An extra chair has appeared. No. 6 (D1): He's taken off his shirt. No. 7 (D4): And *he*'s put on suspenders. No. 8 (E2): Watch it—there's a hole in the lawn. **Did you find the secret bonus difference? If not, log on to** *www.LIFE.com* **to find out what it is.**

Page 41: **Houston, I'll Have a Sandwich** No. 1 (A1): The colors on his headgear have been reversed. No. 2 (A2 to B3): The valve has arrows all around it. Nos. 3 and 4 (B3): The valve handle is now red, and, golly, that is one big tube. No. 5 (C2): His microphone has swelled in size. No. 6 (C5): His name has been changed to LUCAS. No. 7 (D5): *Mmm,* sandwich.

Page 42: **Give Yourself a Star . . .** No. 1 (A1 to B1): The door has been painted pink. No. 2 (A2 to A3): The poster now says LOVE instead of BELONGS. No. 3 (A5): A poster has disappeared. No. 4 (B5): She has rings on all but one finger. No. 5 (C2): Her shirt's flag has dots instead of stars. No. 6 (C4 to C5): She's changed into a T-shirt. No. 7 (E2): Who left the hairbrush in the bowl of chips? *Eeeww!* No. 8 (E4): One foot now has twice as much cream on it.

Page 44: **Watching Grass Grow** No. 1 (A2): The sign says STOP. No. 2 (B1): How much for that new tomato? No. 3 (B4): The green cup drawn on the top sign is now yellow. No. 4 (C1 to C5): The tabletop has been painted. No. 5 (C2 to C3): Another tray of plants has arrived. No. 6 (C4): Thanks for the birthday card! No. 7 (D1 to D3): The CATGRASS sign has been altered to read CUTGRASS.

Page 45: **You're on a Roll** No. 1 (A1): Get that car off the tracks, please. No. 2 (A3): The *E* in CYCLONE is backward. No. 3 (D2): The lovely lady on the horse's back has vanished. No. 4 (D3): Someone has painted red stripes on the white fence. No. 5 (D4): The trash receptacle is now a mailbox. No. 6 (D5): Where did the flowers go? No. 7 (E4): A large soda has appeared.

Page 46: **Are You Seeing Spots?** No. 1 (A5): Those wings have gone completely brown. No. 2 (B1 to B2): Who's looking a little green? No. 3 (B3): Did anyone drop a coin? No. 4 (C3): A big yellow-and-brown spot is missing. No. 5 (D5 to E5): *Bzzzzz!* No. 6 (E2): That one looks crayon-tastic!

Page 48: **What's the Big Hurry?** No. 1 (A1 to A2): Two white lines have become one. No. 2 (A2 to B2): He'll never get wet with an umbrella that size. No. 3 (A5): That's a jaunty red umbrella, friend. No. 4 (B1): A walker has vanished. No. 5 (B3): The lady in red has lost her stripes. No. 6 (B4): Haven't we seen that new pedestrian somewhere before? No. 7 (C5): Her umbrella's point has been extended. Or maybe that's an antenna. No. 8 (D2): His boots are now yellow. No. 9 (D4): His jeans have picked up a yellow patch. No. 10 (E3 to E4): The blue-and-white umbrella has a fresh batch of thin stripes.

Page 50: **Extra Credit** No. 1 (A1): A plate now has a target on it. Watch out for spitballs. Nos. 2 and 3 (A2): Music class starts at three, and that boy's scroll has gotten longer. No. 4 (A4 to D3): Is it still a string instrument if it's lost its strings? No. 5 (A5): Kudos to whoever nailed that A+. No. 6 (B1): The world may be shrinking, but that globe is growing. No. 7 (B2 to C2): Her shirt's been thoroughly checked. No. 8 (B3): Her tie has flipped in front of her bass. No. 9 (B4): Real men wear bow ties. No. 10 (C2): She's picked up a dollop of orange paint on her palette. No. 11 (C3 to D3): That is one *long* necktie. No. 12 (D5): His model has branched out. No. 13 (E3): Um, where are your socks? No. 14 (E4): His shoe has red stripes. No. 15 (E5): Someone has started laying down floor tile. Looks good.

[MASTER]

Page 54: **Howdy, Puzzle Pardner** No. 1 (A2): The yellow and the purple balloons on the cup have switched places. No. 2 (A3 to A4): The dog on the bag has longer ears. No. 3 (B2): An *H* on the gift bag has rotated 90 degrees. No. 4 (B4): Someone has lit the pink candle. No. 5 (C2): A blue noisemaker has appeared. Nos. 6 and 7 (C3): The cord around the crown of his cowboy hat is longer, and the horseshoe design has flipped. No. 8 (C4): The yellow glasses have lost their flower. No. 9 (D1 to D2): The glittery letter on the fringe is now gold. No. 10 (E3 to E4): His shirt has a new orange stripe.

Page 56: **Office Work** No. 1 (A1): The middle button is yellow. No. 2 (A3): The NO SMOKING sign has an extra red slash. No. 3 (B2): The fire extinguisher has lost its instructions. No. 4 (C2): The magazine has scooted over. No. 5 (D1): A desk drawer handle has been stretched. No. 6 (D2): Yowzah! Watch out for that stapler! No. 7 (D3): How does the gray chair stay up with no legs? No. 8 (D4): The trash can has flipped.

Page 58: **Do You Need Glasses?** No. 1 (A2): A bottle has appeared. No. 2 (B4): A glass has fallen off the middle shelf. No. 3 (C1): The record has spun 90 degrees. No. 4 (C3): His shirt collar has white piping. No. 5 (D3 to E3): The headphone cord now winds behind his back. No. 6 (E2): Part of the wallpaper has come full circle. No. 7 (E3): He's poured himself a shot of something. No. 8 (E5): The red can's white dot has vanished.

Page 59: **Something's Missing Here** No. 1 (A2): The watchtower is unoccupied. Nos. 2 and 3 (B3): The sign now reads LAND, OH! And the rowboat has changed directions. Nos. 4, 5, and 6 (B5): We're down one palm tree, but the wood pilings are reaching higher and another gull has flown into view. No. 7 (D4): Who wears short-shorts? Not that gal. No. 8 (E1): Her board has an extra red stripe.

Page 60: **Special Order** In photo No. 4, the Tabasco sauce is green.

Page 61: **Find Everything You Need?** The dots extend all the way up to the edge of photo No. 5.

Page 62: **Kitchen Confidential**
No. 1 (B4): The *N* in HAMILTON is upside down. No. 2 (C2): The cabinets' knobs have moved down. No. 3 (C5): The top oven's window is bigger. Nos. 4 and 5 (D1): An egg has cracked, and the flour is now ALL-PORPOISE. That seems a little fishy. No. 6 (D2): On the salt canister's label, the rain is no longer pouring. No. 7 (D3): The bowl has surplus Kisses. Nos. 8 and 9 (E2): An extra ball of cookie dough has rolled into view, and where did that cupcake come from?

Page 64: **Don't Bug Out** No. 1 (A3): A new "bull's-eye" dot has appeared. No. 2 (A5): The black spot has grown. No. 3 (B1): The body is now black. No. 4 (B3 to C3): Have you been playing connect the dots? No. 5 (C5): An orange wing's lost its markings. No. 6 (D3): What's up with that 3? No. 7 (D4): The black-and-orange fellow's antennae are longer and thicker.

Page 65: **And Don't Go Off the Deep End** No. 1 (C1): The paddle's handle has grown. Nos. 2 and 3 (C2): Do you think the toy truck on the board is going to cannonball? Maybe, but we doubt that guy's vest is brave enough—it's yella. No. 4 (C4 to D4): The flowers on his shorts are gone. No. 5 (D1 to D3): The decorative tiles at the water's edge have lost their triangles. No. 6 (D2): Where's that duck going in such a hurry? No. 7 (D4): That's a nice smile, Mr. Pool Toy.

Page 66: **Picnic Puzzler** No. 1 (B3): The little girl's hair has fallen in front of her shoulder. No. 2 (B4): He has lost a sock. No. 3 (B5 to C5): But he's gained some piping on his shirt. No. 4 (C3): Who emptied the bowl? No. 5 (D2): Careful—that juice is pretty full. No. 6 (D3): When is an apple more than an apple? When it's a pair. No. 7 (E1): Is that pink lemonade in the bottle? No. 8 (E2): Who couldn't use a little extra bread?

Page 67: **Luggage Mix-Up** No. 1 (B1): His collared shirt is now a turtleneck. No. 2 (B5): His necktie is blue. No. 3 (C2): Her bag has been un-zipped. No. 4 (C3): His sleeve has been stretched to cover his watch. No. 5 (C4): That's not just a hat—it's a clock, too. No. 6 (D2): A second yellow lei has appeared. No. 7 (D5 to E5): Her carry-on has gone from fab floral to blah beige.

Page 68: **A Real Eye-Opener**
No. 1 (A3): That vine is going places. No. 2 (B2): The fourth stake has been chopped down to size. No. 3 (B3): The red and the blue on the painted dot have been reversed. No. 4 (C4): *Someone*'s a little pouty. No. 5 (C5): Those eyes are wide open. No. 6 (D3): The stake has dropped its spotted patch. No. 7 (D4): Mr. Blue has new red buttons. No. 8 (E3): A white splotch on the eighth stake has been painted over.

Page 69: **Dad, Did You See That?**
No. 1 (A1 to A2): The checked umbrella now has yellow squares. No. 2 (A2 to A3): Two umbrellas have swapped places. No. 3 (A4): Another striped umbrella has been planted behind the blue one. No. 4 (B5): Hey, kid—that your beach ball? No. 5 (C1): Look: footprints! No. 6 (C2): The stripe on Dad's swimsuit has moved. No. 7 (D4): One umbrella's reflection has vanished.

Page 70: **Here's a Hot One** Nos. 1 and 2 (A2): The falling figure on the warning sticker has flipped, and the markings on the fireman's helmet have been rearranged. No. 3 (A4): Two lights have swapped places. Nos. 4 and 5 (B2): He's misplaced his walkie-talkie, but he *did* pick up a black stripe on the head of his ax. No. 6 (B5): The truck's *F* is now an *E*. Must be from Dublin. No. 7 (C3): His suspenders have lost a strap adjuster. No. 8 (C5): The *D* in DEPARTMENT is backward. No. 9 (D1): The bottom of his ax handle has turned yellow. No. 10 (E5): His pants have a new white stripe. That's hot.

Page 72: **Unexplained Phenomena**
No. 1 (A1): The spider has gone missing. No. 2 (A5): One purple hat has grown by a few sizes. No. 3 (B2): The wooden pole is shorter. No. 4 (B3): The yellow shirt has lost some of its lettering. No. 5 (C1): The mummy's eyes are now black. No. 6 (C3): SpongeBob's tongue is just hangin' out. No. 7 (C4): Frankenstein has a new set of teeth. No. 8 (D2): The 3 on that pumpkin has been flipped. No. 9 (D5): The witch has no hair. No. 10 (E3): The shoe to the rear has an extra stripe.

Page 73: **Watch for Signs** No. 1 (A3): The sign now reads FUNNLE. Good cake. Bad spelling. No. 2 (B3): Another ZEPPOLES sign has appeared inside the food stand. No. 3 (B5): The two parking signs have flip-flopped. No. 4 (C2): The price has soared to $14. That's inflation for you. Nos. 5 and 6 (D3): Her pants have gotten longer, and a third green stripe has appeared. No. 7 (E2): One of the stroller's rear tires has blown up big-time.

No. 8 (E3): The painted bike figure on the pavement has pedaled away. Did you find the secret bonus difference? If not, log on to *www.LIFE.com* to find out what it is.

Page 74: Lost in Translation No. 1 (A1 to B1): The window's frame is now striped. No. 2 (A3): The arch over the column has vanished. No. 3 (B5): One of the railing's slats has been painted white. No. 4 (C1): The *N* in MONEY has been inverted. No. 5 (C3): The French flag has turned Japanese (we really think so). No. 6 (D1): Horizontal bars have been added to the window. No. 7 (D3): That money slot has gotten much wider. No. 8 (E2): On the yellow sign, the DI before VISAS has disappeared. Did you find the secret bonus difference? If not, log on to *www.LIFE.com* to find out what it is.

Page 76: What's Cooking Here? No. 1 (A2): The curtains are now fully closed. No. 2 (A4): An extra yellow circle has shown up. No. 3 (B4 to B5): Did someone turn out the lights in the RV? Nos. 4 and 5 (C3): Lightning strikes twice (or at least another stripe has appeared), and the bottom vent is gone. No. 6 (E2): The folding stool has lost its shadow. Nos. 7 and 8 (E3): Her pants have gotten a bit longer, plus one of the sandaled feet under the table has walked off.

Page 77: Slumber Party No. 1 (A1): One of the small blue-gray tabs has disappeared. No. 2 (A2): The gap between the two boards is gone. Nos. 3 and 4 (A4): The coffee cup is full, and the pot's handle has grown. No. 5 (C2 to D2): The name JORDAN is marked on the big blue backpack. No. 6 (C5): Why, that flower is yellow. No. 7 (E1): How about a second cup of coffee?

Page 78: Only the Hose Knows No. 1 (A2): Watch out—the UFO is firing its death ray! No. 2 (A3): The telephone pole has grown up (and up). No. 3 (C4): The banana has been eaten. No. 4 (C5): The snake has doubled in size. No. 5 (D2): Jeans are definitely more practical for gardening. No. 6 (E1 to E2): The hose has been shortened. No. 7 (E4): Where'd that other pinecone come from?

Page 80: It All Comes Out in the Wash No. 1 (A3): One red arrow is pointing north. No. 2 (A5): A third light has appeared above the blue awning. No. 3 (B1): The pedestrians on the crossing sign now have feet. No. 4 (C4): The credit card signs have swung around to the other side of the pole. No. 5 (D1): The traffic cone has tipped over. No. 6 (D3): One truck light is on. No. 7 (D4): CAR WASH is now CAR WAS. No. 8 (E2): The license plate has turned green.

Page 81: Look What I Found! No. 1 (A2): Another lightbulb has joined the string. No. 2 (B4 to C4): The cart's frame has extra rungs. No. 3 (C4): That's a bloomin' big flower. No. 4 (D2): She bought a third shoe, just in case. No. 5 (D4): A crack between the floorboards has widened. No. 6 (E1): One of the shirt's white stripes has joined the dark side, forming a black mega-stripe. No. 7 (E5): The sandal has vanished.

Page 82: A Nice, Neat Row No. 1 (A1): Look out—that boat has a crack! Nos. 2 and 3 (A4): The rope behind the man has fallen overboard, and his pole has gone to (two) pieces. No. 4 (A5): Nice new stripe on your hat, pal. No. 5 (C1): Another piece of fruit has appeared. No. 6 (D1): The bag's logo has been erased. No. 7 (D5): The hole in the boat's bottom has widened. No. 8 (E3): One piece of fruit looks a little past its prime. Yuck. Did you find the secret bonus difference? If not, log on to *www.LIFE.com* to find out what it is.

Page 84: Don't Flake Out No. 1 (B2): Mom's snowball has, well, snowballed. No. 2 (B3): Junior has put on a ski mask. No. 3 (B4): A new tree has appeared. No. 4 (B5): A snowbank has piled up next to Dad. No. 5 (C1): Her zipper has vanished. No. 6 (D4): The design on his board has been altered. No. 7 (E3): Her board's round tip has been squared off. No. 8 (E4): Someone has made a snow angel.

Page 85: Under Achievers No. 1 (A2): Another blue balloon has appeared. No. 2 (B1): The hand has been pushed out of view by a longer pole. No. 3 (B4): Where's the rest of that neckline, missy? Oh, there it is. No. 4 (C1): Knock, knock. Who's there? A doorknob. No. 5 (D1): A stuffed puppy is sitting in the chair. No. 6 (D4): Her dress has sprouted a new flower. No. 7 (D5): The pink ribbon has been shortened. No. 8 (E1): Her cuff has gotten poufier.

Page 86: Heavy Lifting No. 1 (A1): Part of the bridge is gone. Think someone bought it? No. 2 (A3 to B3): There's another blue stripe. No. 3 (A5): That extra light pole sure brightens things up. No. 4 (B1): The white square on the blue container has moved down. No. 5 (B5 to C5): The vertical siding on one yellow container is now horizontal. No. 6 (C1 to D1): That brown container seems awfully blue. No. 7 (C3): The white arrows have switched directions. No. 8 (D1): The crane is being shadowed. No. 9 (D2): The hubcap is white. No. 10 (D4): The *M* on the container's side is upside down. No. 11 (E4 to E5): The yellow curb is twice as long.

Page 87: Grin and Bear It No. 1 (A3 to A4): The buggy handle's grip is wider. No. 2 (A5): Ring out the book for 1968, ring in one for 1980. No. 3 (B4): Something has sure opened that bear's eyes. No. 4 (C1): We don't know what it is, but

according to the price tag, it costs $5. No. 5 (C3): The bear in the basket looks much happier. No. 6 (C5): The basket's picked up a bow. No. 7 (D4): The wicker pram has lost an axle. No. 8 (E1): Four paving stones have joined as one.

Page 88: Rain, Rain, Go Away The pedestrian in the upper-right corner of photo No. 5 has vanished.

Page 89: Which Witch Is Which? In photo No. 1, the witch's nose is orange.

Page 90: Tool Time No. 1 (A3): The yellow flashlight has a switch. No. 2 (B1): The holes in the electrical socket are different. Nos. 3 and 4 (B3): The *X* on the upside-down can is now an *O*, and the smudges on the wall have united to form a stick figure. No. 5 (B5): A white can has turned yellow. No. 6 (C1): The brush has been swept away. No. 7 (C4): The right handgrip has been extended. No. 8 (D5): The dustpan has flipped. No. 9 (E5): The bike's light has disappeared.

Page 92: Try This On for Size No. 1 (A1): The window is gone. No. 2 (B1): One set of blue and orange balls has swapped places. No. 3 (B2): Her mirror image is wearing a black hat. Nos. 4, 5, and 6 (B3): The mirror has moved over, a girl's face now appears in it, and the plant on the mantel has sprouted a new shoot. No. 7 (B4): Another dress has been hung on the rack. No. 8 (C2 to D2): The sink's drain has been re-routed to the floor. No. 9 (C3): Her black dress is no longer strapless. No. 10 (C4): He has lost his watch. No. 11 (C5 to D5): The radiator is color-coordinated with the walls. No. 12 (D2): The top layer of the dress's trim has vanished. No. 13 (E3): The rug has an extra purple square. No. 14 (E4): The openings in the grate are twice as wide. No. 15 (E5): Some lucky soul has walked off with the pink sash.

[EXPERT]

Page 96: Buoy, That's a Tough One No. 1 (A1): The light-blue handle is longer. No. 2 (A3): The *E* in MAINE on the red-and-white buoy is backward. Nos. 3 and 4 (A4): The small blue-and-white one says MAINE, too, and the yellow handle has a white bottom. No. 5 (C1): The natural-wood buoy now has a white price tag. No. 6 (C2): There's more blue in the color scheme on the large float. No. 7 (D4): Two nails are better than one. No. 8 (E1): The big orange one has lost its price tag. No. 9 (E4): The blue-on-blue job has picked up a—surprise!—blue stripe.

Page 98: Change of Style No. 1 (A5): A flower on the fifth boot over has gone from white to pink. No. 2 (B3): The dowel has been extended. No. 3 (D1): The mannequin head is blushing. No. 4 (D2): The T-shirt's groovy design has a few new splotches. No. 5 (D3): Two gold leaves have been clipped from the wallpaper. No. 6 (D4): The shelf now has a middle bracket. No. 7 (E4): The swirl-patterned boot on the right has an orange toe. No. 8 (E5): A spot has gone missing from that last pair.

Page 99: This One's No Picnic No. 1 (A4 to A5): The sandy baseball diamond has blended into the green grass. No. 2 (A5): Her earring has a new hoop. No. 3 (C1): Someone's stuck a sticker on that banana. No. 4 (C3): Who refilled the Cheetos? No. 5 (C4): One of the tablecloth's white squares has gone red. No. 6 (D2): And so has the tip of the mustard bottle. No. 7 (D3): Double the salt equals double the fun. No. 8 (D4): A corn holder has been unplugged.

Page 100: Flying Colors No. 1 (A2): Another blue feeder disk has appeared. No. 2 (A5): The DO NOT DISTURB sign has moved up. No. 3 (B1): The butterfly is fluttering upside down. No. 4 (B5): Her shirt no longer has a V-neck. No. 5 (C2): A butterfly has alighted in the center of the spiky plant. No. 6 (D4): The red bloom has an extra petal. No. 7 (E4): A long leaf now hangs over the rope. Nos. 8 and 9 (E5): The fence has gained a post, and the sign's middle paragraph is a few lines shorter.

Page 101: What Are You Two Hiding? No. 1 (B1): The lampshade has a second stripe. No. 2 (B3): Must be high tide now in the painting. No. 3 (B5): The lamp's neck has lost its switch. No. 4 (C1): The photo has inched away from the lamp. No. 5 (C2): His belt buckle has become square (but, rest assured, he hasn't). No. 6 (C4): The pattern on the couch's back has gained a flower. No. 7 (E1): The end table is missing a leg. No. 8 (E2): One sock has slipped down. No. 9 (E5): Where'd the power cord go?

Page 102: Make a Wish The red *H* on the blue present in photo No. 6 has rotated 90 degrees.

Page 103: Find the Spare Change In picture No. 3, the American flag in the left window has thicker red stripes.

Page 104: **Squeeze Play** No. 1 (A2): His necklace has slipped off. No. 2 (B2): The spoon's handle has a hole in it. Nos. 3 and 4 (C1): Another cup of lemonade has been tucked behind that half-full one, and an extra lemon has appeared. No. 5 (C2): The faintest red tablecloth stripe—between the *A* and the *D* in LEMONADE—is now darker. No. 6 (C4): The pink and the fuchsia stripes between her arms have been reversed. No. 7 (D2): The *D* on the sign is now a capital letter. No. 8 (D4): The cup has fallen off the wagon. No. 9 (E5): That rear wheel picked up nifty red detailing.

Page 105: **Take a Fresh Look** No. 1 (A2): PROUD TO BAKE? No, PROUD TO BE. No. 2 (A3): The word MEATS has lost its *S*. No. 3 (B1): The Visa and the MasterCard logos have swapped places. No. 4 (B4): One handle, good; two handles, even better. Nos. 5 and 6 (C2): The red dolly has an extra bar, and the spinach has been piled higher. No. 7 (C3): The third crate has lost its handhold. No. 8 (E5): The last crate has three new nail holes.

Page 106: **Easter Egg Hunt** No. 1 (A2): Three new stems have sprouted. No. 2 (A3): Hey there, extra yellow chick. No. 3 (A4): Another egg has become speckled. No. 4 (B3): A white jelly bean has turned big and red. No. 5 (B5): The fuzzy slipper at right has lost its stitching. No. 6 (C4): The dark egg's center design—sort of looks like the top of a wheat stalk—has been inverted. No. 7 (D1): Who took a bite out of that leaf? No. 8 (D4): The chick-on-a-stick has raised its wing. No. 9 (E3): The brown egg is upside down.

Page 108: **What's Up, Dock?** No. 1 (A2): A quarter of the grate has disappeared. No. 2 (A3): The cart has an extra white bar. No. 3 (A5): The *R* and the *P* on the forklift have switched places. No. 4 (B1): The cart hitch has vanished. No. 5 (B2): The front cart's shadow has grown. No. 6 (B4): The shadow of the topmost velvet rope is gone. No. 7 (C5): The wooden ramp has extended itself. No. 8 (D2): A sixth light-blue package has appeared. No. 9 (E2): The man has backed up. No. 10 (E5): The rail has veered off.

Page 110: **Garden of Surprises** No. 1 (A2): A bird has landed on the telephone pole. No. 2 (A3): A wire has vanished. No. 3 (B1): The UFO is AWOL. No. 4 (C2): The crown of her hat has gotten higher. Nos. 5 and 6 (C3): The center of the biggest flower is now black, and the largest leaf has six additional veins. No. 7 (C4): The boy's chinstrap has fallen behind his shoulder. No. 8 (D2): Her jacket now has a breast pocket. Nos. 9 and 10 (D5): The soccer ball has a new pattern, while the clock's minute hand has jumped 10 minutes. No. 11 (E2): Nice to meet you, second ladybug! Did you find the secret bonus difference? If not, log on to *www.LIFE.com* to find out what it is.

Page 112: **Fully Loaded** No. 1 (A1): The spring on the rear door has been stretched. No. 2 (B2): The rearview mirror is camouflaging itself among the trees. No. 3 (B4): A black horizontal line has appeared on the kid's hat. No. 4 (B5): One of the boat's blue stripes is lighter. No. 5 (C2): That T-shirt sleeve is longer. No. 6 (C4 to D5): The basketball's red and white stripes have swapped places. No. 7 (D4): The suitcase's right corner has lost its little protective plate. No. 8 (E1): The taillight is more orange, less red.

Page 113: **You'd Better Not Cry** No. 1 (A4): A gold pot has flipped upside down. No. 2 (B1): The horizontal paneling trim has moved down. No. 3 (B3): The mantel's red ribbon garnish has grown longer on one side. No. 4 (C2 to D2): Santa's white jacket stripe has shifted over. No. 5 (C5): A tree ornament has vanished. Maybe Prancer couldn't hold out for the carrot. No. 6 (D1): Teddy's sticking out his tongue. Careful, Ted—he knows when you've been bad or good. No. 7 (E3): Santa's boot has new red stripes. No. 8 (E4): The rug's rectangular design has dropped a line. No. 9 (E5): The frayed fringe has been repaired.

Page 114: **The Party's Over** No. 1 (A1): The champagne flute has been refilled. No. 2 (A4): That glass now holds pink bubbly. No. 3 (A5): The tabletop has an extra white divider. No. 4 (B1): The blue party popper has rolled away. No. 5 (C4): Formerly dotty, the cardboard kerchief is now a little square. No. 6 (D4): Is that a ring in the glass of wine? No. 7 (D5): The beer has extra foam. No. 8 (E1): The floor's been vacuumed.

Page 115: **Pick Up the Tempo** No. 1 (A2 to B2): A picture has crept up the wall. No. 2 (B1): Did someone move the flowers? Nos. 3 and 4 (B5): Lightning is striking in the painting. Meanwhile, the two topmost flags on the model ship have swapped places. No. 5 (C2): His pants have an extra belt loop. No. 6 (D1): The bottom leaf has doubled in size. No. 7 (D5): Two little drawers have become one big drawer. No. 8 (E3): Is he stepping on her toes? Ouch!

Page 116: **Pouring It On** No. 1 (A1): The window is shorter by one board width. No. 2 (A3): Another purple bloom has blossomed. No. 3 (A5): The birdhouse has a second round opening. No. 4 (B1): The smiling gnome figurine suddenly looks perturbed. Nos. 5 and 6 (B2): The bird's-nest decoration has migrated south, and the butterfly has tilted in the opposite direction. No. 7 (B4): His shirt has lost part of its print. No. 8 (C3): The spiky plant has dropped some foliage. No. 9 (D2): The happy statue's hair ribbon has moved from one side to the other. No. 10 (D4): The planter has an extra foot. Did you find the secret bonus difference? If not, log on to *www.LIFE.com* to find out what it is.

Page 118: More Fun Than a Movie
No. 1 (A4): The starburst popcorn sign has moved right. No. 2 (A5): The ice cream truck has a flat tire. No. 3 (B2): The word CORN on one box is upside down. No. 4 (B3 to B4): The capital and the lowercase *P*'s in the neon popcorn sign have flip-flopped. No. 5 (B5): He's slipped on an undershirt. No. 6 (C4): Where'd her thumb ring go? No. 7 (C5): Watch out for falling popcorn! No. 8 (D1): A white flower on his shirt has grown. No. 9 (D5): There's an extra pack of yellow candy, if you want one. No. 10 (E2): He now has two bracelets.

Page 120: One Tough Cookie
No. 1 (A3): The ceiling light has vanished. Nos. 2 and 3 (B2 to C2): Mom's apron has inched up, and the apple on its front has a third leaf. No. 4 (B3): The colors in the poster's checkerboard floor have been reversed. No. 5 (B4): A bottle on the side counter got recycled. No. 6 (C3): The pear on Sis's apron has flipped over. No. 7 (D2): Another cookie has appeared on the Crisco can. Nos. 8, 9, and 10 (D3): That milk looks a bit chocolaty—perhaps because one of the Kisses is missing. Plus, the *I* in JIF is now capitalized. No. 11 (E5): The dough ball at the far right has rolled to the left. **Did you find the secret bonus difference?** If not, log on to *www.LIFE.com* to find out what it is.

Page 122: Sink or Swim No. 1 (A2): A branch has grown longer. No. 2 (B3): The hole in the clouds is no more. No. 3 (C3): The diving board's rail has an extra post. No. 4 (C5): The action figure has traded camo for slimming black. Nos. 5 and 6 (D2): He has a new arm tattoo, and he's pulled up his swimsuit. No. 7 (D3): The toy motorcycle has switched directions. No. 8 (D4): He's put on one white sock. No. 9 (D5): The inflatable duck's now looking up. No. 10 (E4): The turtle has crawled toward the goggles.

[GENIUS]

Page 126: This Paint's Been Mixed
In photo No. 2, the top two spots on the right side of the black-and-white fence post have swapped places.

Page 127: Can You Catch It? Her sleeve in picture No. 3 is almost long enough to cover her watch.

Page 128: A Little Bit of Everything
No. 1 (A2): That drawer needs to get a handle. No. 2 (A3): Did someone leave an extra spoon around here—in the salad bowl, perhaps? No. 3 (A4): That guest's dress has lost some leaves. No. 4 (B3): Looks like we used less salad dressing than we thought. No. 5 (B4): The bread pictured on the box of croutons is now whole wheat. No. 6 (C2): Who left their keys on the table? No. 7 (C5): She's painted her red nails green. No. 8 (D2): How's it going, Mr. Peanut? No. 9 (D3): Someone's cleaned up the ice cream lid. No. 10 (E1): The bowl has an extra red dot.

Page 129: Race Against Time
No. 1 (A1): The yellow CAR is now a yellow CAB. No. 2 (B3): The stripes on the red Mustang's hood have fused together. No. 3 (C2): A red hash mark on the truck has disappeared. No. 4 (C3 to C4): The Mustang's shadow has cleared up. No. 5 (C5): The road on the billboard has become a passing zone—check out the yellow line. No. 6 (D2): The hood ornament is leaning back. No. 7 (D4): His armband has moved up his forearm. No. 8 (E3): Where'd his foot go?

Page 130: Now Things Get Interesting
No. 1 (A2): That little bugger's eyes sure are big and beady. No. 2 (B1): The name NINA has appeared on a wing. No. 3 (B4): There's a black ring around that one's lower-left "bull's-eye." No. 4 (C2): The dark spot inside the lower right oval on that brown-and-orange butterfly has moved down. Nos. 5 and 6 (C4): The faintly blue guy has lost his tail, while three dots have disappeared from the wing in front of Mr. Lost-His-Tail. No. 7 (D2): A happy little face smiles from that brown-and-white one. No. 8 (D3): The pencil-thin stripes on the dark-brown wings have been erased. No. 9 (E1): The "eyes" in the bottom left corner are now looking left. No. 10 (E5): His white stripes have gone gray.

Page 132: One Really Hard Bargain
No. 1 (A1): A ceiling pipe's been extended. No. 2 (A4): The wire on which a mirror hangs has vanished. No. 3 (B2): The dollar sign has two lines instead of one. No. 4 (B3): There's another gray frame. No. 5 (B4): An empty frame has been filled with dark gray. No. 6 (C1): The black-and-white wall poster is now white-and-black. No. 7 (C2): The shadow on the red pillar has gotten longer. No. 8 (C4): The reflection of the office chair shows an extra foot. No. 9 (D3): The box's yellow label has moved down. No. 10 (E3): A package of frames is a bit fuller.

Page 134: Final Exam No. 1 (A1): The window is shorter. No. 2 (A4): The long-haired girl has on a blue headband. No. 3 (A5): There's a napkin and flatware on the right rear table. No. 4 (B1): A brown table has turned orange. Nos. 5 and 6 (B2): Someone has thrown away his lunch, and the boy's white shirt has lost a stripe. Nos. 7, 8, and 9 (B3): A purple drink has gravitated toward the table's edge. The boy in the blue T-shirt is now holding a fork, and his headband has been straightened. No. 10 (B5): His khaki pants have become olive drab. No. 11 (C1): A napkin has vanished. No. 12 (C2): Her pants have a pink stripe. No. 13 (C3): Her blue pen has rolled toward her other hand. No. 14 (C5): The foot under the table has walked off. No. 15 (D1): Her peas and carrots have switched spots. No. 16 (D3): Her juice box now has a straw. No. 17 (D5): His collar has a new blue button. No. 18 (E3): The holes in her sheet of paper have switched sides. Nos. 19 and 20 (E4): Someone has scratched JF + CS into the tabletop. And give that boy extra carrots. So, did you pass?